Plato was a philosopher and mathematician. He was known for being the Greek philosopher that assisted with forming the Western philosophy foundation and founding the Academy in Athens, Greece. In this book, we will learn more about his lifetime trials and tribulations.

GROWING UP IN ATHENS

Plato was born in Athens, Greece 427 BC. He was raised in this Greek city-state during the Classical Period of Ancient Greece. While historians may not know much about his early life, they do know that he came from a wealthy family and probably had one sister and two brothers. He would have learned from the best teachers about varying subjects that included philosophy, grammar, math, gymnastics and music.

PLATO

A Man of Mysterious Origins Biography Book 4th Grade Children's Biography Books

BABY PROFESSOR
EDUCATION KIDS

Speedy Publishing LLC
40 E. Main St. #1156
Newark, DE 19711
www.speedypublishing.com
Copyright 2017

Plato

Athenian Army

THE PELOPONNESIAN WAR

Much of his youth would have been affected by the Peloponnesian War between Sparta and Athens. More than likely, Plato would have served during his early life in the Athenian army, and this war no doubt would have influenced his philosophy and life.

SOCRATES

As he grew older, Plato became more interested in philosophy and academics. He became a close follower and student of the well-known philosopher Socrates. Socrates would spend time in conversation with students about various aspects of life and politics. They would then proceed to break the problem down and come up with theories regarding the subject. These teachings and learning styles became the foundation of Plato's writings.

Socrates

Death of Socrates

STUDY AND TRAVEL

Socrates was executed in 399 BC by Athens' leaders for corrupting their youth and for not acknowledging Athens' gods. Plato then left Athens to travel around the Mediterranean region the following 12 years. During this time period, he visited locations such as North Africa, Egypt and Italy. He studied many subjects that included philosophy, math and science.

THE DIALOGUE

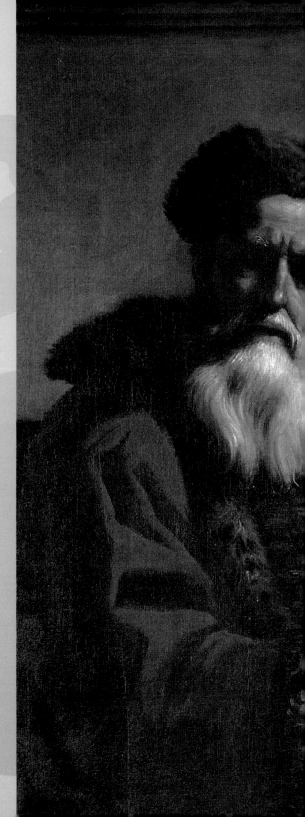

As he was traveling the Mediterranean, he started writing and wrote in an intriguing style referred to as a "dialogue", where he would introduce many characters that would discuss a subject by asking questions to each other.

This format allowed him to explore many sides of an argument as well as introducing new ideas.

Diogenes and Plato

Several of his dialogues featured Socrates, his former teacher, as the main character. Most of what we know about Socrates' philosophies are learned from Plato's dialogues. Plato wrote four dialogues regarding the finals days of Socrates, which includes The Apology, where Socrates' defends himself prior to his death sentence.

THE REPUBLIC

The Republic is Plato's most famous writing. In this writing, numerous characters debate the meaning of justice and how it is related to our happiness. Once again, Socrates in the key character in these dialogues and he talks about how being just or unjust has an effect on a person's life.

Plato

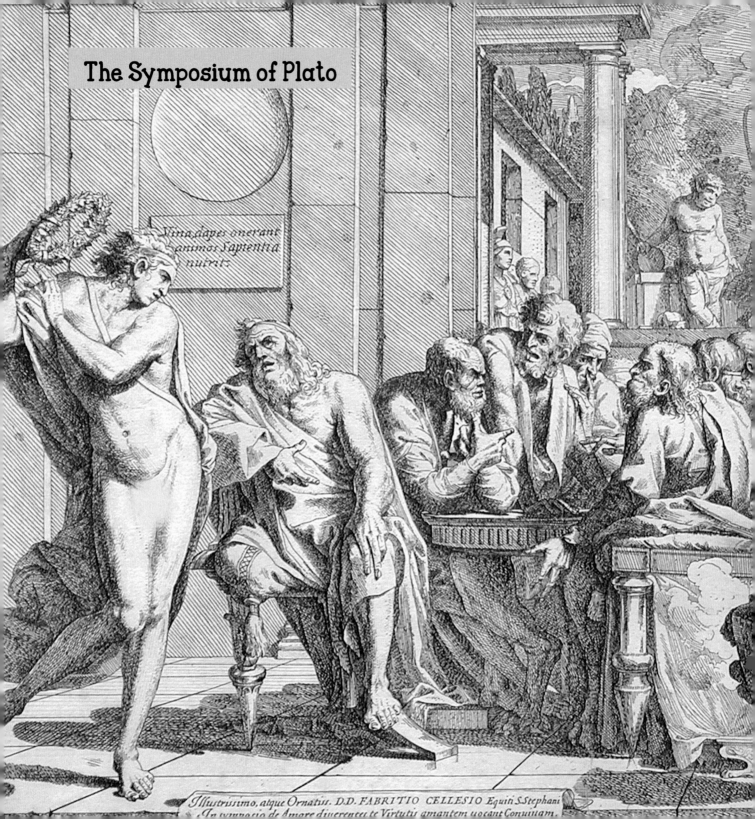

The Symposium of Plato

Vina dapes onerant
animos Sapientia
nutrit.

Illustrissimo, atque Ornatiss. D.D. FABRITIO CELLESIO Equiti S.Stephani
In symposio de Amore disserentes te Virtutis amantem vocant Conuiuam.

Also discussed are various aspects of the government and finally presented as the ideal ruler is the "philosopher-king". Plato then realizes that kings must become philosophers, or philosophers must become kings.

THE ACADEMY

When he was about 40, Plato returned home to Athens and started a school named the Academy. He and other professors would teach subjects including astronomy, biology, philosophy, and mathematics at this school. One of his students who studied there for about 20 years was Aristotle, the famous philosopher and scientist.

Plato and Aristotle

PLATO'S DEATH AND LEGACY

Plato passed away in Athens around 347 BC. There is not much information available regarding his death, however, he was 80 years old and more than likely passed away in his sleep. His legacy lives on in the modern Western philosophy world and his writings have been studied for the past 2000 years and continue to be studied today at universities.

GREEK PHILOSOPHERS

Greek philosophers were known as "seekers and lovers of wisdom", and would analyze and study the world surrounding them using reason and logic. While philosophy is often thought of as a religion or "the meaning of life", these philosophers were also known to be scientists. Many had also studied physics and mathematics. They would often be teachers of wealthy children and some of the more notable ones would open their own academies or schools.

Socrates

SOCRATES

Socrates was a philosopher born in Athens, Greece in 469 BC and is most well-known for helping to form the foundation of Western Philosophy.

Socrates did not write his ideas and thoughts down like some of the other famous Greek philosophers. He preferred simply speaking to his followers. Plato and Xenophon, two of his students, however, wrote about Socrates.

Xenophon

Xenophon

We learn about his philosophies in several of Plato's dialogues where Socrates is a key character and takes part in many philosophical discussions. As a historian, Xenophon wrote about Socrates' life events. Additionally, we have learned about Socrates from Aristophanes' Greek plays.

SOCRATES' EARLY LIFE

Not much information is available regarding his early life. His father, Sophroniscus, was a stonemason and his mother was a midwife. He did come from a wealthy family and more than like did not have much formal education. Socrates started working with his father as a stonemason early in his career.

Socrates

Socrates

SOCRATES THE SOLDIER

Socrates lived during the Peloponnesian War between the city-states of Sparta and Athens. He was required to fight since he was a male citizen of Athens and served as a foot soldier known as a "hoplite". He would have used a spear and large shield for fighting. He fought in many battles and became noted for his valor and courage.

SOCRATES THE TEACHER AND PHILOSOPHER

As he grew older, he started exploring philosophy. He focused on ethics and how a person should behalf rather than focusing on the physical world. He believed that happiness stemmed from leading a life of good morals rather than having material possessions and encouraged people to pursue goodness and justice other than power and wealth. These ideas were very radical for this time period.

Socrates Drinking the Hemlock

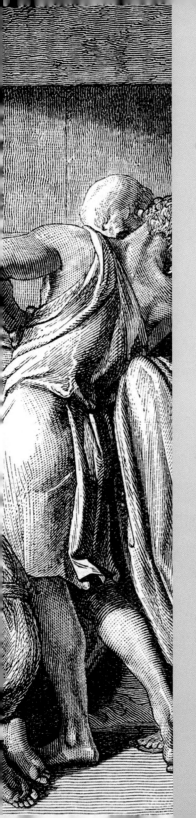

Scholars and young men of Athens started gathering around Socrates for philosophical discussions. Discussions would include ethics as well as Athens' current political issues. He chose to not provide answers to these questions, but posed questions and discussed possible answers. Other than claim that he knew all the answers, he would say "I know that I know nothing".

THE SOCRATIC METHOD

He had a very unique way to teach and explore different subjects by asking questions and then discussing possible answers. These answers would then pose additional questions and would lead to a better understanding of the subject. The logical process of using questions and answers so as to learn about a subject is what is known today as the Socratic Method.

Stone Statue of Socrates

SOCRATES' TRIAL AND DEATH

Once Athens lost to Sparta during the Peloponnesian War, a group of men known as the Thirty Tyrants took over power. One of its leading members was one of Socrates students by the name of Critias. Soon, the men of Athens rose to the occasion and the Thirty Tyrants were replaced with a democracy.

Socrates was branded a traitor since he spoke against the democracy and the leader of the Thirty Tyrants was one of his students. He went to trial for "failing to acknowledge the gods of the city" and "corrupting the youth". The jury convicted him and he was sentenced to death by consuming poison and died in Athens Greece 399 BC.

The Death of Socrates

Aristotle

HIS LEGACY

Considered to be one of the founders of the modern Western philosophy, Socrates' teachings have influenced future Greek philosophers including Aristotle and Plato. His philosophies continue to be studied in today's world and the Socratic Method is used across the world in modern-day law schools and universities.

OTHER GREEK PHILOSOPHERS

Aristotle

ARISTOTLE

Even though he was a student of Plato, Aristotle did not necessarily agree with everything Plato said and he liked focusing more on the practical areas of philosophy, such as science. He started the Lyceum, his own school. He felt that reason was the greatest good and felt it important to maintain self-control. He was a tutor of Alexander the Great.

PYTHAGORAS

He is most well-known for his Pythagorean Theorem which people use for finding the length of the sides of right triangles. In addition, he felt that the world was centered on mathematics.

Pythagoras

Epicurus

EPICURUS

He believed gods had no interest in human beings and that we should be happy and enjoy our lives. He taught that pain and pleasure are how good and evil are measured; death is the end of both our body and our soul and we should not fear it; he believed that the gods neither punish or reward humans; that the universe is eternal and infinite; and that events occur ultimately due to the interactions and motions of atoms that move through an empty space.

ZENO

Zeno founded the philosophy referred to as Stoicism and that happiness was the result of accepting whatever would happen, whether it be good or bad. His philosophy emphasized that a person's actions were more important than their words.

Zeno of Citium

Ancient Greek Authors

Now that you have learned about Greek philosophers, which one do you find you have the most in common with? Who would you have liked to study with?

For more information about these famous Greek philosophers you can go to your local library, research the internet, and ask questions of your teachers, family and friends.

Visit

BABY PROFESSOR
EDUCATION KIDS

www.BabyProfessorBooks.com

to download Free Baby Professor eBooks
and view our catalog of new and exciting
Children's Books

Made in the USA
Coppell, TX
22 April 2020